# Science

## PaRragon

Bath · New York · Singapore · Hong Kong · Cologne · Delhi · Melbourne

Author: Steve Parker

This edition published by Parragon in 2009
Parragon
Queen Street House
4 Queen Street
Bath BA1 1HE, UK

ISBN 978-1-4075-7665-7
Printed in China

# Contents

# Bony bits

Your bones are strong and hard. They hold up the softer parts of your body. Your muscles move your bones. All of your bones together are called your skeleton.

## Bone shapes

Different bones have different shapes. The longest bone is your upper leg, or thigh bone. The widest bone is your hip. The main bone inside your head is your skull.

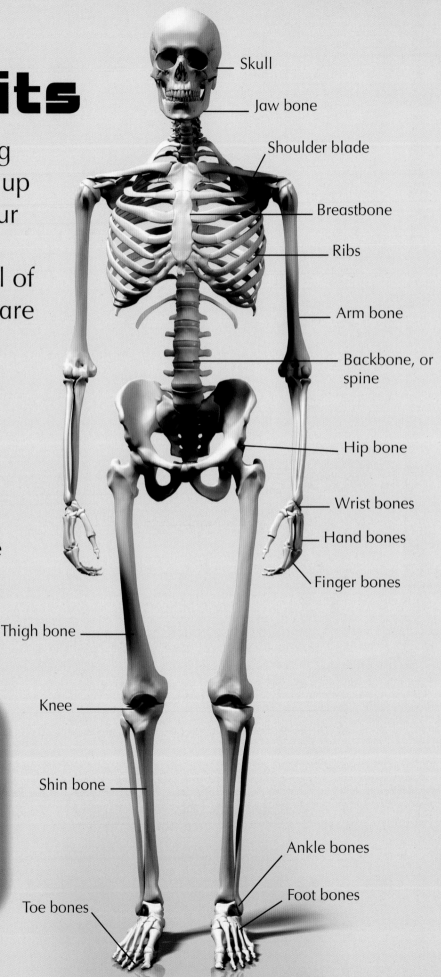

Skull

Jaw bone

Shoulder blade

Breastbone

Ribs

Arm bone

Backbone, or spine

Hip bone

Wrist bones

Hand bones

Finger bones

Thigh bone

Knee

Shin bone

Ankle bones

Foot bones

Toe bones

## Did you know?

A young baby has about 350 bones. As it grows, some of the bones join together. This is why an adult has only 206 bones.

# Hip joint

At the point where your thigh meets your hip there is a joint called a ball joint. This allows the thigh bone to move in almost every direction.

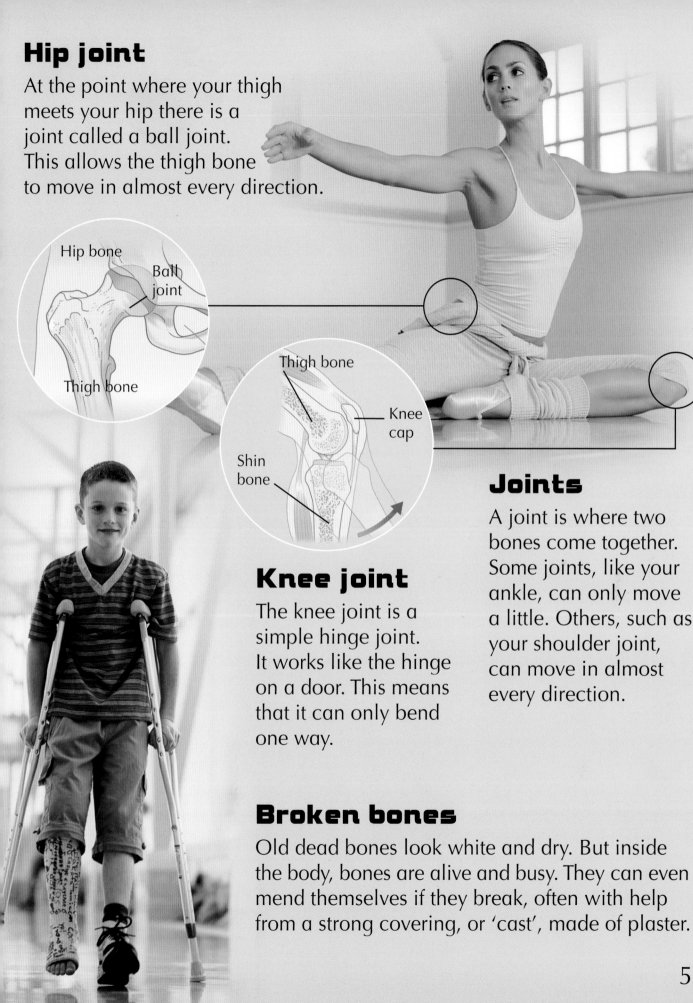

Hip bone

Ball joint

Thigh bone

Thigh bone

Knee cap

Shin bone

# Knee joint

The knee joint is a simple hinge joint. It works like the hinge on a door. This means that it can only bend one way.

# Joints

A joint is where two bones come together. Some joints, like your ankle, can only move a little. Others, such as your shoulder joint, can move in almost every direction.

# Broken bones

Old dead bones look white and dry. But inside the body, bones are alive and busy. They can even mend themselves if they break, often with help from a strong covering, or 'cast', made of plaster.

# Muscles

Every time you move, you use your muscles. Even when you are sitting still, your muscles are busy working. You are still breathing and blinking, and your heart carries on beating. All of these actions use muscles.

## Powerful muscles

Muscles come in all shapes and sizes. Some muscles are large and powerful. Lifting weights makes your muscles stronger.

Shoulder muscle

Arm muscles

## Did you know?

You have hundreds of muscles in your body – in fact, about 640. Your muscles make up almost half your body weight.

The biggest muscle is in the buttock (bottom).

## Muscle power

Most muscles are joined to a bone at each end. When the muscle gets shorter, it pulls on the bones and makes your joints move. Usually several muscles pull together for each movement.

The large muscle in your lower leg is called the calf muscle.

The smallest muscle is inside the ear.

## Tireless legs

Athletes who run long distances have longer, thinner muscles than weightlifters. These muscles may not be so big, but they can keep working for much longer. This helps the athletes to run long races without tiring.

The longest muscle is across the front of the leg.

## Face it

You have more than 60 muscles in your head and around your eyes, nose and mouth. You use these to make your face move. Try looking surprised, happy or sad. Can you feel the muscles working?

# Breathing

What do you do all the time, yet hardly ever think about? You breathe – in and out, all day and all night. This is because your body needs a gas called oxygen, which is in the air all around you.

## Breathing in, breathing out

As you breathe in, air flows into two spongy bags in your chest called lungs. Your lungs take in the oxygen from the air and release the waste carbon dioxide gas, which you breathe out.

## Puffer

People with an illness called asthma often need to use an inhaler, or puffer, to help them breathe more easily.

Your lungs are like two balloons that fill with air when you breathe in.

Snorkel

# Air

You need to breathe air all the time. So if you swim under water you either have to hold your breath or breathe through a tube called a snorkel.

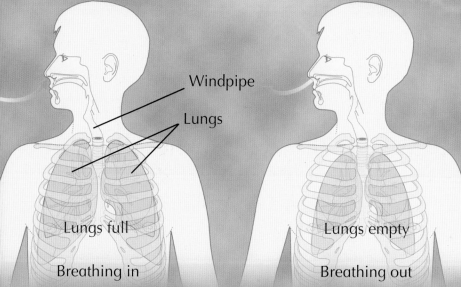

Windpipe

Lungs

Lungs full

Breathing in

Lungs empty

Breathing out

# Voice box

When you talk, sing or shout, you use your voice box. Air coming up the windpipe from your lungs shakes the voice box to make the sounds. Opera singers train their voices so they can sing loudly.

# The lungs

You normally breathe in and out through your nose. As you breathe |in, the ribs in your chest move upwards and outwards. Air passes down your windpipe and fills up your lungs. When you breathe out, your chest moves downwards and inwards, pushing the air out of your lungs.

# Blood

Blood flows all around your body. Pumped by the heart, it never stops moving. Its main job is to carry oxygen, and special substances from food, all around your body.

## Blood vessels

Blood vessels are the tubes that carry blood all around the body. Arteries are blood vessels carrying blood with fresh oxygen. Veins carry blood containing waste carbon dioxide.

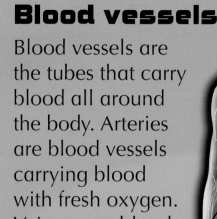

Heart

Artery

Vein

## Testing blood

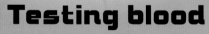

Sometimes when you are ill a nurse may take a few drops of your blood for a test. Blood often carries germs or other signs of illness that can help a doctor understand why you are unwell.

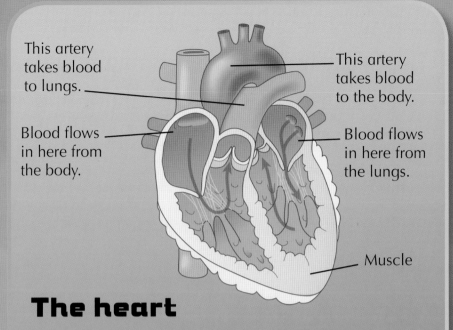

This artery takes blood to lungs.

This artery takes blood to the body.

Blood flows in here from the body.

Blood flows in here from the lungs.

Muscle

## The heart

The heart is a large muscle. It works like a pump, sucking blood in and then pushing it out. The left side of the heart pumps the blood around the body. The right side of the heart pumps the blood around the lungs.

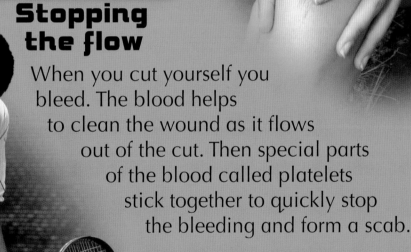

## Stopping the flow

When you cut yourself you bleed. The blood helps to clean the wound as it flows out of the cut. Then special parts of the blood called platelets stick together to quickly stop the bleeding and form a scab.

## Healthy heart

The heart is a muscle, so one way to keep it healthy and strong is to do any kind of exercise that makes it beat faster. Even when you are resting your heart beats about 70–80 times a minute. But when you do sport it can beat twice as fast.

# Your brain

If you could see inside your head, then you might think that your brain was not very exciting. It looks like pink-grey jelly. But your brain is really quite amazing, because it controls your whole body. It is also where you think, have ideas, learn and remember.

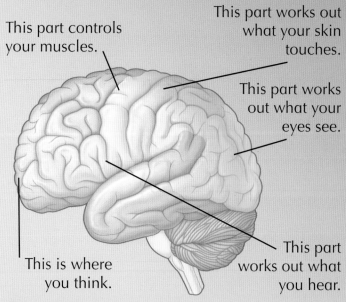

This part controls your muscles.

This part works out what your skin touches.

This part works out what your eyes see.

This is where you think.

This part works out what you hear.

## Brain parts

Different parts of your brain do different jobs. The brain also has two sides. The left side controls the right side of your body, and the right side controls the left side of your body.

## Left-handed

Most people prefer to write or throw a ball with their right hand. We call them right-handed. But about one person in ten is left-handed. There are more left-handed boys than girls.

## Pain

When you hurt yourself, your nervous system sends messages to the brain to tell it you are in pain. The brain makes you feel pain to warn you that there is a problem.

## Problem solving

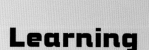

To play a game like chess, you use your brain in lots of ways. You have to learn and remember how to move the pieces. Then you have to work out what will happen next when you make a move.

## Learning

To learn you need to remember things. Your brain can store and find things more quickly than the biggest computer. To play music you have to remember what the notes mean and where to put your fingers to play them.

13

# Energy

Energy is the ability to make things happen, move or change. There are many kinds of energy, including light, heat, electricity and sound. One kind of energy can also change into another.

## Energy for life

You need energy to run, jump, shout, breathe and even think. All your energy comes from the food that you eat. Your stomach breaks down the food to unlock the energy stored inside it.

This car has solar panels that make electricity to drive its wheels.

## Energy from the Sun

Heat from the Sun warms the air, land and sea. Plants use the energy in sunlight to make their own food. Sunlight can also be turned into electricity using solar panels.

## Food energy

Sugary foods give us instant energy. Starchy foods, such as pasta, bread and rice, release their energy more slowly, and keep us going for longer.

## Movement energy

Things that move very fast, such as the wind, have a lot of energy. A wind turbine has propeller-like blades that turn in the wind. The turning blades drive a generator that produces electricity.

## Fuel energy

Fuels are energy-rich substances that we burn for light and heat, and to power machinery. Coal, oil and gas are called fossil fuels. They formed millions of years ago from the remains of dead plants and animals.

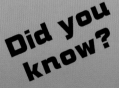
An oil rig pumps oil from under the sea floor.

### Did you know?

The Sun's energy makes life on Earth possible. Heat and light take just over eight minutes to travel from the Sun's surface to the Earth.

# Solid, liquid, gas

Substances can exist in three different forms. Solids keep their shape and size. Liquids can flow and change shape, but they cannot be squeezed smaller. Gases can flow and change shape. They can also be squeezed smaller or spread out bigger.

## Different water

Liquid water flows in rivers and oceans. Water also exists as solid ice, and as a gas called steam.

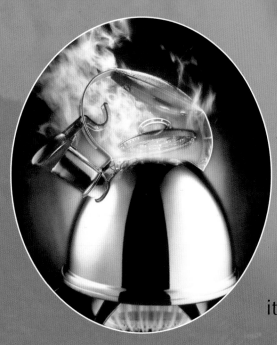

## From liquid to gas

When we heat water in a kettle or a saucepan, bubbles of gas form in the water and escape as steam. This change from a liquid into a gas is called evaporation. When a gas cools and turns back into a liquid, it is called condensation.

# Floating on air

Air is a mixture of gases, such as nitrogen, oxygen and carbon dioxide. Some other gases weigh less than the gases in air. This airship is filled with a gas called helium. Helium is lighter than air, so the airship floats.

Airships only need small engines as they are so light.

## Did you know?

If you squeeze a gas smaller, it gets hotter. This is why a bicycle pump becomes warm when you pump up a tyre.

# Melt and freeze

If a solid is heated enough it will turn into a liquid. This is called melting. A glass-blower makes vases by blowing air into melted glass. When the glass cools, it becomes solid again.

This glass is so hot it glows red. Heat makes it soft so it can be shaped.

# Down to Earth

People often wish they could fly like birds. But we are kept on the ground by the Earth's gravity. This is a downward force that pulls on everything – even birds, which is why they must flap their wings to stay in the air.

## Falling fast

When skydivers jump out of a plane, they fall very fast. This is because gravity pulls them down to the ground. When their parachutes open, they catch the air, so the skydivers fall more slowly.

## Beating gravity

As a plane moves along the runway, the air rushing over its wings makes an upward force called lift. When lift is greater than the force of gravity, the plane takes off.

# Earth's gravity

Everything has gravity – including you! You pull on the Earth, just as the Earth pulls on you. But gravity depends on size. You are quite small, so your gravity is weak. The Earth is huge, so it has very strong gravity.

Away from the Earth's gravity, out in space, everything floats about as if it were weightless.

## Did you know?

A rocket has to reach a certain speed to break free of the Earth's gravity and get into space. This speed is called 'escape velocity'. It is 300 times faster than a car speeding along a motorway!

# Sliding down

The force of gravity is at work in the playground, too. It is gravity that pulls you down a slide. The steeper the slide, the faster you go.

# Simple machines

Machines make it easier for us to do things, or help us do things we could not do at all. Some of the most useful machines, like ramps, levers and wheels, are also really simple.

## Ramps

Ramps are sometimes used instead of stairs or escalators. They help people to move from one level to another. They are useful for people with wheelchairs, luggage or baby buggies.

## Gears

Gears are the toothed wheels that your bicycle chain wraps around. Usually there is one big gear wheel attached to the pedals, and one or more smaller gear wheels attached to the back wheel. Having gears of different sizes at the back makes it easier for you to ride your bicycle up and down hills.

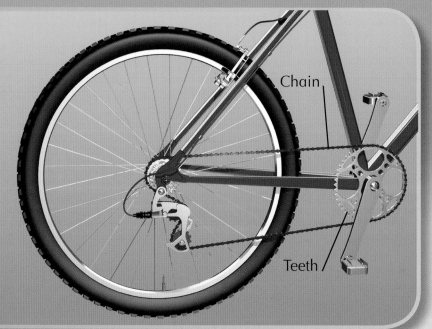

Chain

Teeth

# Wheels

Wheels help us to move or carry heavy loads. Some wheels are tiny. Others are over 3 metres high. Bigger wheels make it easier for heavy trucks to travel over rough ground without getting stuck in the mud.

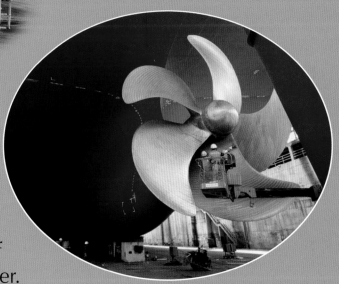

# Screws and propellers

The screw is a simple machine. As you turn a wood screw with a screwdriver it pulls its way into the wood. A ship's propeller is also a kind of screw. But it pushes, instead of pulls, the ship through the water.

# Levers

To use a lever you have to rest it on something. The point where it rests is called the fulcrum.

A lever can help us to lift things that would usually be too heavy for us. The see-saw is a lever that allows you to lift your partner into the air.

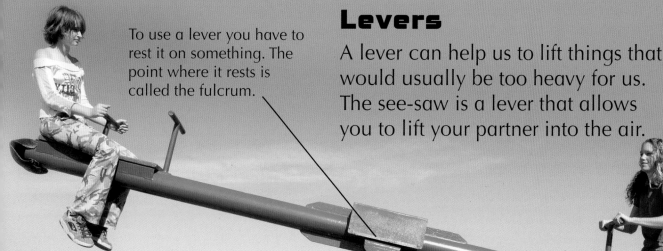

21

# On the road

Our roads are busy with machines we call vehicles. These include cars, motorcycles, trucks and buses. They take people, loads and cargoes from one place to another.

This electric car is not only quiet and clean, it also goes very fast.

## Electric cars

Most cars have petrol or diesel engines. An electric car has big batteries that power an electric motor. It is quiet and wastes less energy than a petrol-engined car.

## Bendy buses

Bendy buses are like two buses joined together. They can carry more people around crowded cities – but they only need one driver.

## On two wheels

A motorbike is small and fast. But it can only carry one or two people. Some racing bikes can travel at over 300 kilometres an hour.

## Articulated lorries

The biggest lorries are called articulated lorries. They have a separate cab and engine at the front, called a tractor, and a big load-carrying trailer at the back.

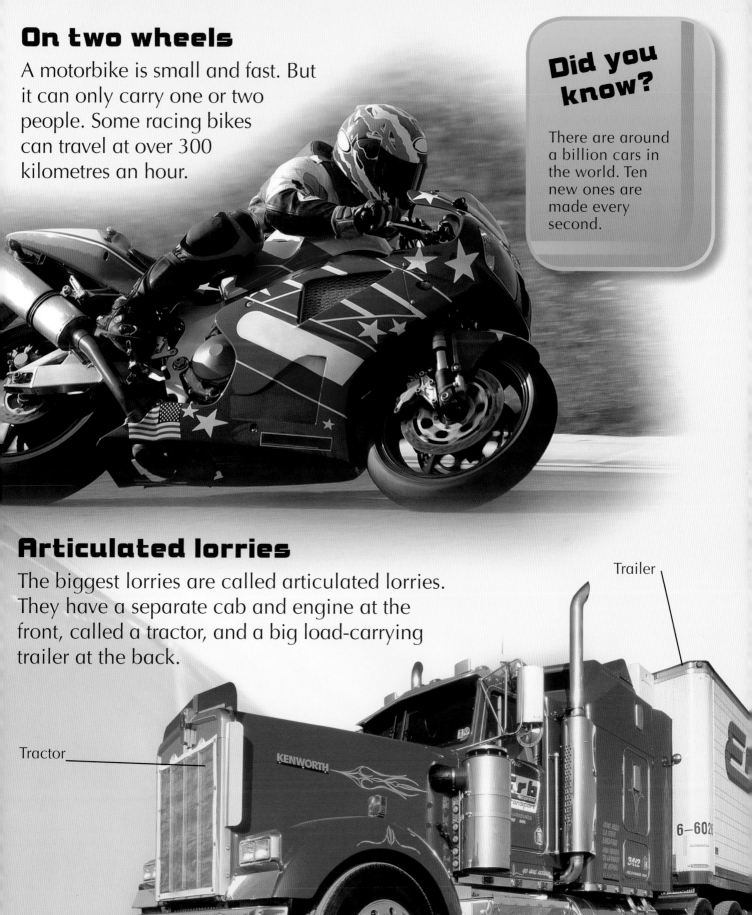

Trailer

Tractor

# Acknowledgements

Artwork:
**David Lewis Illustration:** 5TR Bruce Hogarth, 7C,TL Bruce Hogarth, 9C Bruce Hogarth, 11TL Bruce Hogarth, 12TR Bruce Hogarth;
**Precision Illustration:** 20BR Tim Loughhead

Photo credits:
b – bottom, t – top, r – right, l – left, m – middle

Cover: Front – Joe Drivas/GettyImages, back – Anatole Branch/GettyImages, StockTrek/GettyImages.

Poster: Dreamstime.com/Anthony Hathaway.

Internals:
**Alvey & Towers:** 22BR; **Corbis:** 30TR Reuters, 4BR Rob Lewine, 5B Zefa/Joson, 6R Zefa/Matthias Kulka, 7BL Jim Craigmyle,
7TR Zefa/Gary Salter, 8TR Roy Morsch, 8B Tom & Dee Ann McCarthy, 9TR Stephen Frink, 9BR epa/Marcos Delgado,
10CL dpa/Maurizio Gambarini, 12BL Jim Erickson, 13TR Reuters, 13CL Reuters/Stringer, 14C Larry Williams, 14BL Reuters/Reuters,
14–15BRBL epa/British Petroleum, 15TL Tom & Dee Ann McCarthy, 15R Visuals Unlimited, 16BL James Noble, 18BL George Hall,
19BR Tom & Dee Ann McCarthy, 21B Zefa/Ole Graf, 21TL Lester Lefkowitz, 21CR TWPhoto, 22TL Reuters/Issei Kato,
23B Zefa/Kurt Amthor; **Getty Images:** 1C Bill Reitzel, 10–11BRBL Taxi/Jim Cummins, 11TR Iconica/PM Images,
13BR Stone/Don Smetzer, 16C Photodisc Green/Robert Glusic, 17B Science Faction/Louie Psihoyos, 18C Photonica/Roberto Mettifogo,
20TL Taxi/Dana Neely; **iStockPhoto:** 4TL Macroworld, 6TL Macroworld, 8TL Macroworld, 10TL Macroworld, 12TL Macroworld,
17TR Charles Shapiro, 20TL Alvaro Heinzen, 22TL Alvaro Heinzen, 23TL Andrea Leone; **Science Photo Library:** 10TR Alfred Pasieka;
**Scintilla Pictures:** 4BL John Avon.